D1400955

Frances Ros

soups

simple and delicious easy-to-make recipes

This is a Parragon Publishing Book
This edition published in 2004

Parragon Publishing
Queen Street House
4 Queen Street
Bath, BA1 1HE, UK

Copyright © Exclusive Editions 2002

ISBN: 1-40543-862-2

Printed in China

Produced by
THE BRIDGEWATER BOOK COMPANY LTD

Photographer Calvey Taylor-Haw
Home Economist Ruth Pollock

Cover Photographer Mark Wood
Home Economist Cover Pamela Gwyther

NOTES FOR THE READER

- This book uses both imperial and metric measurements. Follow the same units of measurement throughout; do not mix imperial and metric.

- All spoon measurements are level: teaspoons are assumed to be 5 ml, and tablespoons are assumed to be 15 ml.

- Unless otherwise stated, milk is assumed to be whole milk, eggs and individual vegetables such as potatoes are medium, and pepper is freshly ground black pepper.

- Recipes using raw or very lightly cooked eggs should be avoided by infants, the elderly, pregnant women, convalescents, and anyone suffering from an illness.

- The times given are an approximate guide only. Preparation times differ according to the techniques used by different people and the cooking times may also vary from those given. Optional ingredients, variations, or serving suggestions have not been included in the calculations.

contents

introduction

There is no substitute for good, homemade soup, and creating soups at home can be a tremendously enjoyable experience. You need very little in the way of basic cooking equipment, just a large pan with a lid and a sharp knife for chopping. A large skillet or wok is also helpful, but not essential.

Soup can be very economical to make—you can use leftovers to make some delicious concoctions, from light appetizers and snacks to more substantial soups that are meals in themselves. On special occasions, you can splash out on more expensive ingredients and create impressive soups that will grace any dinner table.

Soups are very nutritious, too, and can be packed with healthy ingredients such as vegetables, fish, beans, and rice. Many are low in fat, and high-fat ingredients such as cream can be replaced with lower fat alternatives.

pea & mint soup
page 14

bouillabaisse
page 42

Soup is also a popular international food. Many of the recipes included in this book reflect the rich diversity of the different cuisines found across the world, so wherever you happen to be—and whatever the occasion— you are bound to find something in its pages to satisfy your taste and delight your dinner guests.

easy

Recipes are graded as follows:
1 spoon = easy;
2 spoons = very easy;
3 spoons = extremely easy.

serves 4

Recipes generally serve four people. Simply halve the ingredients to serve two, taking care not to mix metric and imperial measurements.

10 minutes

Preparation time. Where marinating or soaking are involved, these times have been added on separately: eg, 15 minutes + 30 minutes to marinate.

10 minutes

Cooking time. Cooking times do not include the cooking of side dishes or accompaniments served with the main dishes.

turkey & lentil soup
page 58

spicy lentil soup
page 76

Vegetables are very healthy foods and make nutritious, satisfying ingredients in soups. The combinations of texture and flavor in this section are endless. From the chilled Gazpacho, with its ripe tomatoes and red bell peppers, to the delightful Vegetable Soup with Pesto, packed with fresh basil and garlic, there are mouthwatering recipes for every season using every type of vegetable. Alcohol is also a great favorite in soups, so why not try the Mushroom & Sherry Soup? And for cheese lovers, the Sweet Potato & Stilton Soup cannot be missed.

vegetable soups

gazpacho

very easy   serves 4

15 minutes   none
+ 2–3 hours
to chill

1 lb 2 oz/500 g large ripe tomatoes
4 tbsp extra-virgin olive oil
3 scallions, trimmed and chopped
2 red bell peppers, seeded
  and chopped
3 garlic cloves, chopped
1 cucumber, peeled and chopped
1 tbsp red wine vinegar
1 tbsp chopped mixed herbs
salt and pepper

GARNISH
croûtons (see page 24)
sprigs of fresh basil
fresh crusty rolls, to serve

First, skin the tomatoes. Bring a pot of water to a boil, put the tomatoes into a heatproof bowl, then pour over enough boiling water to cover them. Let soak for about 3 minutes, then lift the tomatoes out of the water and let cool slightly. When they are cool enough to handle, gently pierce the skins with the point of a knife. Remove and discard the skins.

Cut the tomatoes in half and remove the seeds. Chop the flesh and put it into a food processor. Add the oil, scallions, bell peppers, garlic, cucumber, vinegar, and mixed herbs to the food processor. Season with salt and pepper and blend until smooth. Push the blended mixture through a strainer into a large bowl, then cover with plastic wrap and refrigerate for 2–3 hours.

Ladle the chilled soup into serving bowls and garnish with croûtons and sprigs of fresh basil. Serve with fresh crusty rolls.

vichyssoise

very easy   serves 4

15–20 minutes + 2¼ hours to cool/chill   35 minutes

ingredients

2 tbsp butter
2 shallots, chopped
2 large leeks, trimmed and sliced
1 lb/450 g potatoes, peeled and diced
1 tbsp chopped fresh chives
1 bay leaf
2½ cups vegetable bouillon
salt and pepper
½ cup light cream

GARNISH
swirl of light cream
chopped fresh chives
fresh crusty rolls, to serve

Melt the butter in a large pan over medium heat. Add the shallots and cook, stirring, for 2 minutes, until slightly softened. Add the leeks and cook, stirring, for another 2 minutes. Add the potatoes, chives, bay leaf, and bouillon, and season with salt and pepper. Bring to a boil, then reduce the heat, cover the pan, and simmer for 30 minutes. Remove from the heat and let the soup cool for 15 minutes.

Remove and discard the bay leaf, then transfer the soup into a food processor and blend until smooth (you may need to do this in batches). Transfer into a large bowl and stir in the cream. Cover with plastic wrap and chill in the refrigerator for at least 2 hours.

When ready to serve, remove from the refrigerator and ladle into serving bowls. Garnish each bowl with a swirl of cream and some chopped fresh chives and serve with fresh crusty rolls.

leek & potato soup

very easy   serves 4

15–20
minutes
+ 10 minutes
to cool

35 minutes

ingredients

2 tbsp butter
2 garlic cloves, chopped
3 large leeks, trimmed and sliced
1 lb/450 g potatoes, peeled and
    chopped into bite-size chunks
1 tbsp chopped fresh parsley
1 tbsp chopped fresh oregano
1 bay leaf
3½ cups vegetable bouillon
salt and pepper

generous ¾ cup crème fraîche or
    plain yogurt
3½ oz/100 g smoked firm cheese, such as
    Applewood, grated

GARNISH
chopped fresh parsley
fresh chives

thick slices of fresh crusty bread,
    to serve

Melt the butter in a large pan over medium heat. Add the garlic and cook, stirring, for 1 minute. Add the leeks and cook, stirring, for another 2 minutes. Add the potatoes, herbs, and bouillon, and season with salt and pepper. Bring to a boil, then reduce the heat, cover the pan, and simmer for 25 minutes. Remove from the heat, let cool for 10 minutes, then remove and discard the bay leaf.

Transfer half of the soup into a food processor and blend until smooth (you may need to do this in batches). Return to the pan with the rest of the soup, stir in the crème fraîche, and reheat gently. Season with salt and pepper.

Remove from the heat and stir in the cheese. Ladle into serving bowls and garnish with chopped fresh parsley and chives. Serve with thick slices of fresh crusty bread.

pea & mint soup

very easy   serves 4

15 minutes   40 minutes
+ 10 minutes
to cool

ingredients

1 tbsp butter

3 shallots, chopped

2 leeks, trimmed and finely chopped

1 potato, peeled and chopped

1 lb/450 g frozen peas

2 tbsp chopped fresh mint

3½ cups vegetable bouillon

salt and pepper

sprigs of fresh mint, to garnish

slices of fresh whole-wheat bread, to serve

Melt the butter in a large pan over medium heat. Add the shallots and cook, stirring, for 2 minutes. Add the leeks and cook, stirring, for another 2 minutes. Add the potato, peas, chopped mint, and bouillon, and season with salt and pepper. Bring to a boil, then reduce the heat, cover the pan, and simmer for 30 minutes. Remove from the heat and let cool for 10 minutes.

Transfer the soup into a food processor and blend until smooth (you may need to do this in batches). Return to the pan, season with salt and pepper, and reheat gently.

Remove from the heat and pour into individual serving bowls. Garnish the soup with sprigs of fresh mint and serve with slices of fresh whole-wheat bread.

creamy carrot & parsnip soup

very easy   serves 4

15–20 minutes + 10 minutes to cool

55 minutes – 1 hour

4 tbsp butter
1 large onion, chopped
1 lb/450 g carrots, peeled and chopped
2 large parsnips, peeled and chopped
1 tbsp grated fresh gingerroot
1 tsp grated orange zest
2½ cups vegetable bouillon
½ cup light cream
salt and pepper

GARNISH
light cream
sprigs of fresh cilantro
fresh crusty rolls, to serve

Melt the butter in a large pan over low heat. Add the onion and cook, stirring, for 3 minutes, until slightly softened. Add the carrots and parsnips, cover the pan, and cook, stirring occasionally, for about 15 minutes, until the vegetables have softened a little. Stir in the gingerroot, orange zest, and bouillon. Bring to a boil, then reduce the heat, cover the pan, and simmer for 30–35 minutes, until the vegetables are tender. Remove the soup from the heat and let cool for 10 minutes.

Transfer the soup into a food processor and blend until smooth (you may need to do this in batches). Return the soup to the pan, stir in the cream, and season well with salt and pepper. Warm through gently over low heat.

Remove from the heat and ladle into soup bowls. Garnish each bowl with a swirl of cream and a sprig of fresh cilantro and serve with fresh crusty rolls.

mushroom & sherry soup

very easy   serves 4

15 minutes   40 minutes

ingredients

4 tbsp butter

2 garlic cloves, chopped

3 onions, sliced

1 lb/450 g mixed white and chestnut
   mushrooms, sliced

3½ oz/100 g fresh cèpes or porcini
   mushrooms, sliced

3 tbsp chopped fresh parsley

generous 2 cups vegetable bouillon

salt and pepper

3 tbsp all-purpose flour

½ cup milk

2 tbsp sherry

½ cup sour cream

GARNISH

sour cream

chopped fresh parsley

fresh crusty rolls, to serve

Melt the butter in a large pan over low heat. Add the garlic and onions and cook, stirring, for 3 minutes, until slightly softened. Add the mushrooms and cook for another 5 minutes, stirring. Add the chopped parsley, pour in the bouillon, and season with salt and pepper. Bring to a boil, then reduce the heat, cover the pan, and simmer for 20 minutes.

Put the flour into a bowl, mix in enough milk to make a smooth paste, then stir it into the soup. Cook, stirring, for 5 minutes. Stir in the remaining milk and the sherry and cook for another 5 minutes. Remove from the heat and stir in the sour cream. Return the pan to the heat and warm gently.

Remove from the heat and ladle into serving bowls. Garnish with sour cream and chopped fresh parsley, and serve the soup with crusty rolls.

vegetable soup with pesto

very easy   serves 4

20 minutes   45 minutes

ingredients

2 tbsp olive oil
2 garlic cloves, chopped
2 onions, chopped
1 celery stalk, trimmed and chopped
1 carrot, peeled and chopped
5 cups vegetable bouillon
1 potato, peeled and chopped
6 oz/175 g frozen peas
14 oz/400 g canned cannellini beans
salt and pepper
1 tbsp chopped fresh basil

PESTO

2 garlic cloves, chopped
1 oz/25 g fresh basil leaves
generous 3/4 cup grated Parmesan
  cheese
5 tbsp extra-virgin olive oil
generous ¾ cup pine nuts
sprigs of fresh basil, to garnish

fresh focaccia, to serve

Heat 2 tablespoons of olive oil a large pan over low heat. Add the garlic and onions and cook, stirring, for 3 minutes, until slightly softened. Add the celery and carrot and cook for another 5 minutes, stirring. Pour in the bouillon, then add the potato, peas, and beans. Season with salt and pepper. Bring to a boil, then reduce the heat, cover the pan, and simmer for 30 minutes.

Meanwhile, to make the pesto, put all the ingredients into a food processor and blend until smooth.

Stir the chopped basil into the soup and cook for another 5 minutes. Remove from the heat and ladle into serving bowls. Garnish each bowl with a generous tablespoonful of pesto and a sprig of basil, and serve with fresh focaccia.

asparagus & lemon soup

very easy serves 4

15–20 minutes
+ 10 minutes
to cool

40 minutes

ingredients

2 tbsp butter
3 leeks, trimmed and sliced
1 celery stalk, trimmed and sliced
5 cups vegetable bouillon
1 tbsp finely grated lemon zest
2 tbsp lemon juice
1 potato, peeled and chopped
1 tbsp chopped fresh parsley

salt and pepper
1 lb/450 g young, tender asparagus,
    cut into 1-inch/2.5-cm pieces
½ cup light cream

fine strips of lemon zest, to garnish

fresh crusty rolls, to serve

Melt the butter in a large pan over medium heat. Add the leeks and cook, stirring, for 3 minutes, until slightly softened. Add the celery and cook for another 3 minutes, stirring. Add the bouillon, lemon zest and juice, potato, and parsley, and season with salt and pepper. Bring to a boil, then reduce the heat, cover the pan, and simmer for 25 minutes. Add the asparagus and cook for another 5 minutes. Remove from the heat and let cool for 10 minutes.

Transfer half of the soup into a food processor and blend until smooth. Return to the pan with the rest of the soup, stir in the cream, and reheat gently.

Remove from the heat and ladle into serving bowls. Garnish with fine strips of lemon zest and serve with fresh crusty rolls.

onion soup with croûtons

very easy · serves 4

15–20 minutes · 1 hour

ingredients

scant ½ cup butter
2 garlic cloves, crushed
3 large onions, thinly sliced
1 tsp sugar
2 tbsp all-purpose flour
scant 1 cup dry white wine
6¼ cups vegetable bouillon
salt and pepper

CROUTONS
2 tbsp olive oil
2 slices day-old white bread,
    crusts removed

slices of fresh whole-wheat and white
    bread, to serve

Melt the butter in a large pan over medium heat. Add the garlic, onions, and sugar and cook, stirring, for about 25 minutes, until the onions have caramelized.

In a bowl, mix the flour with enough wine to make a smooth paste, then stir it into the onion mixture. Cook for 2 minutes, then stir in the remaining wine and the bouillon. Season with salt and pepper. Bring to a boil, then reduce the heat, cover the pan, and simmer for 30 minutes.

Meanwhile, to make the croûtons, heat the oil in a skillet until hot. Cut the bread into small cubes and cook over high heat, stirring, for about 2 minutes, until crisp and golden. Remove from the heat, drain the croûtons on paper towels, and set them aside.

When the soup is cooked, remove from the heat and ladle into serving bowls. Scatter over some fried croûtons and serve with slices of whole-wheat and white bread.

italian tomato soup

very easy   serves 4

20 minutes   50–55
+ 10 minutes   minutes
to cool

ingredients

2 tbsp extra-virgin olive oil

2 large garlic cloves, crushed

1 large onion, chopped

2 lb/900 g ripe vine tomatoes, skinned
(see page 8), seeded, and coarsely
chopped, juices reserved

generous 1¾ cups vegetable bouillon

salt and pepper

4 tbsp chopped fresh basil

4 tbsp mascarpone

sprigs of fresh basil, to garnish

TO SERVE

small slices of fresh ciabatta

thinly sliced mozzarella

Heat the oil in a large pan over medium heat. Add the garlic and onion and cook, stirring, for about 2 minutes, until slightly softened. Add the tomatoes and their juices and cook for another 3 minutes, then pour in the bouillon and season with salt and pepper. Bring to a boil, then lower the heat, cover the pan, and simmer for about 35–40 minutes. Remove from the heat and let cool for 10 minutes.

Transfer half of the soup into a food processor and blend until smooth. Return to the pan with the rest of the soup, stir in the chopped basil, and cook for another 5 minutes. Stir in the mascarpone and heat through briefly.

Remove from the heat and ladle into serving bowls. Garnish with sprigs of fresh basil and serve with slices of ciabatta topped with thin slices of mozzarella.

sweet potato & stilton soup

very easy   serves 4

15–20
minutes
+ 10 minutes
to cool

45 minutes

ingredients

4 tbsp butter
1 large onion, chopped
2 leeks, trimmed and sliced
6 oz/175 g sweet potatoes, peeled
  and diced
3½ cups vegetable bouillon
1 tbsp chopped fresh parsley
1 bay leaf

pepper
⅔ cup heavy cream
5½ oz/150 g Stilton cheese, crumbled

2 tbsp finely crumbled Stilton cheese,
  to garnish

thick slices of fresh bread, to serve

Melt the butter in a large pan over medium heat. Add the onion and leeks and cook, stirring, for about 3 minutes, until slightly softened. Add the sweet potatoes and cook for another 5 minutes, stirring, then pour in the bouillon, add the parsley and the bay leaf, and season with pepper. Bring to a boil, then lower the heat, cover the pan, and simmer for about 30 minutes. Remove from the heat and let cool for 10 minutes. Remove and discard the bay leaf.

Transfer half of the soup into a food processor and blend until smooth. Return to the pan with the rest of the soup, stir in the cream, and cook for another 5 minutes. Gradually stir in the crumbled Stilton until melted (do not let the soup boil).

Remove from the heat and ladle into serving bowls. Garnish with finely crumbled Stilton and serve with slices of fresh bread.

Fish and shellfish are very nutritious and quick to cook. Many are low in calories and fat, yet rich in protein and nutrients such as B vitamins. They are also an excellent source of iodine, which helps to maintain a healthy thyroid gland and keeps the metabolism running efficiently. Above all, however, fish and shellfish are delicious, and impart a marvelous richness to soups. Always buy the freshest you can find, and you will be rewarded with soups that are unparalleled in terms of quality and flavor.

seafood soups

traditional salmon soup

extremely easy

serves 4

15 minutes

40 minutes

ingredients

2 tbsp butter
1 onion, chopped
1 leek, trimmed and sliced
1 tbsp all-purpose flour
generous 2¾ cups fish bouillon
1 large potato, peeled and chopped
1 tbsp chopped fresh parsley
1 tbsp chopped fresh dill

salt and pepper
10½ oz/300 g skinless salmon fillets,
    cut into bite-size pieces
2 egg yolks
scant ½ cup heavy cream
sprigs of fresh dill, to garnish

slices of crusty bread, to serve

Melt the butter in a large pan over medium heat. Add the onion and leek and cook, stirring, for 3 minutes, until slightly softened. In a bowl, mix the flour with enough bouillon to make a smooth paste and stir it into the pan. Cook, stirring, for 1 minute, then gradually stir in the remaining bouillon with the potato, parsley, and dill. Season with salt and pepper. Bring to a boil, then lower the heat, cover the pan, and simmer for 25 minutes.

Add the salmon to the pan and cook for about 6 minutes until cooked through. In a clean bowl, whisk together the egg yolks and cream, then stir into the soup.

Remove from the heat and ladle into serving bowls. Garnish with sprigs of fresh dill and serve with slices of crusty bread.

tuna chowder

very easy   serves 4

15–20 minutes   50 minutes

ingredients

2 tbsp butter

1 large garlic clove, chopped

1 large onion, sliced

1 carrot, peeled and chopped

2½ cups fish bouillon

14 oz/400 g potatoes, peeled and cut into
   bite-size chunks

14 oz/400 g canned chopped tomatoes

14 oz/400 g canned cannellini
   beans, drained

1 tbsp tomato paste

salt and pepper

1 zucchini, trimmed and chopped

8 oz/225 g canned tuna in
   brine, drained

1 tbsp chopped fresh basil

1 tbsp chopped fresh parsley

scant ½ cup heavy cream

sprigs of fresh basil, to garnish

thick slices of whole-wheat bread, to serve

Melt the butter in a large pan over low heat. Add the garlic and onion and cook, stirring, for 3 minutes, until slightly softened. Add the carrot and cook for another 5 minutes, stirring. Pour in the bouillon, then add the potatoes, tomatoes, beans, and tomato paste. Season with salt and pepper. Bring to a boil, then reduce the heat, cover the pan, and simmer for 20 minutes.

Add the zucchini, tuna, and chopped basil and parsley and cook for another 15 minutes. Stir in the cream and cook the soup very gently for another 2 minutes.

Remove from the heat and ladle into serving bowls. Garnish with sprigs of fresh basil, and serve with slices of whole-wheat bread.

cullen skink

extremely easy serves 4

15 minutes 40 minutes

ingredients

2 tbsp butter
1 onion, chopped
1 leek, trimmed and chopped
2 tbsp all-purpose flour
3½ cups milk
1 bay leaf
2 tbsp chopped fresh parsley
salt and pepper
12 oz/350 g smoked haddock
   fillets, skinned

1 lb/450 g potatoes, peeled, cooked,
   and mashed
6 tbsp heavy cream
chopped fresh parsley, to garnish

TO SERVE
fresh crusty rolls
fresh salad greens

Melt the butter in a large pan over medium heat. Add the onion and leek and cook, stirring, for about 3 minutes, until slightly softened. In a bowl, mix the flour with enough milk to make a smooth paste and stir it into the pan. Cook, stirring, for 2 minutes, then gradually stir in the remaining milk. Add the bay leaf and chopped parsley and season. Bring to a boil, then lower the heat and simmer for 15 minutes.

Rinse the haddock fillets under cold running water, drain, cut into bite-size chunks, and add them to the soup. Cook for 15 minutes, until the fish is tender and cooked right through. Add the mashed potatoes and stir in the cream. Cook for another 2–3 minutes, then remove from the heat and discard the bay leaf.

Ladle into serving bowls, garnish with chopped fresh parsley, and serve with fresh crusty rolls and fresh salad greens.

haddock & shrimp chowder

very easy   serves 4

20 minutes   40 minutes

ingredients

1 tbsp butter
1 onion, chopped
3 tbsp all-purpose flour
generous 2 cups fish bouillon
1 bay leaf
salt and pepper
generous 2 cups milk
2 tbsp dry white wine
juice and grated zest of 1 lemon
1 lb/450 g haddock fillets, skinned

4½ oz/125 g frozen corn
  kernels, thawed
9 oz/250 g shrimp, cooked and peeled
generous ¾ cup heavy cream
whole cooked shrimp, to garnish

TO SERVE
fresh whole-wheat bread
fresh salad greens

Melt the butter in a large pan over medium heat. Add the onion and cook, stirring, for about 3 minutes, until slightly softened. In a bowl, mix the flour with enough bouillon to make a smooth paste and stir it into the pan. Cook, stirring, for 2 minutes, then gradually stir in the remaining bouillon. Add the bay leaf and season with salt and pepper. Bring to a boil, then lower the heat. Pour in the milk and wine, and stir in the lemon juice and grated zest. Simmer for 15 minutes.

Rinse the haddock under cold running water, then drain, and cut into bite-size chunks. Add them to the soup with the corn. Cook for 15 minutes, until the fish is tender and cooked through. Stir in the shrimp and the cream. Cook for another 2–3 minutes, then remove from the heat and discard the bay leaf.

Ladle into serving bowls, garnish with whole cooked shrimp, and serve with fresh whole-wheat bread and fresh salad greens.

mixed fish soup

very easy   serves 4

20 minutes   40 minutes

ingredients

1 tbsp butter
2 shallots, chopped
1 leek, trimmed and sliced
3 tbsp all-purpose flour
generous 2 cups fish bouillon
1 bay leaf
salt and pepper
generous 2 cups milk
2 tbsp dry sherry
2 tbsp lemon juice
10½ oz/300 g haddock fillets, skinned
10½ oz/300 g cod fillets, skinned

7 oz/200 g canned or freshly
   cooked crabmeat
5½ oz/150 g canned corn
   kernels, drained
generous ¾ cup heavy cream

TO GARNISH
sprigs of fresh dill
wedges of lemon

fresh crusty rolls, to serve

Melt the butter in a large pan over medium heat. Add the shallots and leek and cook, stirring, for about 3 minutes, until slightly softened. In a bowl, mix the flour with enough bouillon to make a smooth paste, then stir it into the pan. Cook, stirring, for 2 minutes, then gradually stir in the remaining bouillon. Add the bay leaf and season with salt and pepper. Bring to a boil, then lower the heat. Pour in the milk and sherry, and stir in the lemon juice. Simmer for 15 minutes.

Rinse the haddock and cod under cold running water, then drain and cut into bite-size chunks. Add to the soup with the crabmeat and corn. Cook for 15 minutes, until the fish is tender and cooked through. Stir in the cream. Cook for another 2–3 minutes, then remove from the heat and discard the bay leaf.

Ladle into serving bowls, garnish with sprigs of fresh dill and lemon wedges, and serve with fresh crusty rolls.

bouillabaisse

easy   serves 4

20 minutes
+ 10 minutes
to soak

45 minutes

ingredients

scant ½ cup olive oil
3 garlic cloves, chopped
2 onions, chopped
2 tomatoes, seeded and chopped
generous 2¾ cups fish bouillon
1¾ cups white wine
1 bay leaf
pinch of saffron threads
2 tbsp chopped fresh basil
2 tbsp chopped fresh parsley

7 oz/200 g live mussels
9 oz/250 g snapper or monkfish fillets
9 oz/250 g haddock fillets, skinned
7 oz/200 g shrimp, peeled and deveined
3½ oz/100 g scallops
salt and pepper

fresh baguettes, to serve

Heat the oil in a large pan over medium heat. Add the garlic and onions and cook, stirring, for 3 minutes. Stir in the tomatoes, bouillon, wine, bay leaf, saffron, and herbs. Bring to a boil, reduce the heat, cover, and simmer for 30 minutes. Meanwhile, soak the mussels in lightly salted water for 10 minutes. Scrub the shells under cold running water and pull off any beards. Discard any with broken shells. Tap the remaining mussels and discard any that refuse to close. Put the rest into a large pan with a little water, bring to a boil and cook over high heat for 4 minutes. Remove from the heat and discard any that remain closed.

When the tomato mixture is cooked, rinse the fish, pat dry, and cut into chunks. Add to the pan and simmer for 5 minutes. Add the mussels, shrimp, and scallops, and season. Cook for 3 minutes, until the fish is cooked through. Remove from the heat, discard the bay leaf, and ladle into serving bowls. Serve with fresh baguettes.

seafood soup

easy   serves 4

15 minutes   35 minutes
+ 10 minutes
to soak

ingredients

2 lb 4 oz/1kg live mussels

⅔ cup dry white wine

2 tbsp butter

1 onion, sliced

1 leek, trimmed and sliced

3½ cups water

pinch of saffron threads

9 oz/250 g snapper fillets, skinned

9 oz/250 g haddock fillets, skinned

1¼ cups heavy cream

1 tbsp cornstarch

7 oz/200 g shrimp, peeled
 and deveined

3½ oz/100 g scallops

salt and pepper

sprigs of fresh dill, to garnish

fresh whole-wheat rolls, to serve

Soak the mussels in salted water for 10 minutes. Scrub under cold running water; pull off any beards. Discard any with broken shells and any that refuse to close when tapped. Put the rest into a pan with the wine; bring to a boil. Cook over high heat for 4 minutes. Discard any that remain closed. Let cool. Lift out the mussels and remove the shells. Strain the cooking liquid and reserve. Melt the butter in a pan over medium heat. Add the onion and leek. Cook, stirring, for 3 minutes. Stir in the water, saffron, and cooking liquid. Bring to a boil, lower the heat, and simmer for 15 minutes.

Rinse the fish fillets, pat dry, and cut into small chunks. Add to the pan and simmer for 5 minutes. Stir in the cream. Blend the cornstarch in 2 tablespoons of water and stir into the soup. Add the shrimp and scallops, season, and cook for 2 minutes. Add the mussels and cook for 1 minute. Remove from the heat and ladle into serving bowls. Garnish the soup with sprigs of dill and serve with fresh whole-wheat rolls.

crab & vegetable soup

very easy · serves 4

15–20 minutes · 40 minutes

ingredients

2 tbsp chili oil
1 garlic clove, chopped
4 scallions, trimmed and sliced
2 red bell peppers, seeded
  and chopped
1 tbsp grated fresh gingerroot
4 cups fish bouillon
salt and pepper
scant ½ cup coconut milk
scant ½ cup rice wine or sherry
2 tbsp lime juice

1 tbsp grated lime zest
6 kaffir lime leaves, finely shredded
10½ oz/300 g freshly cooked crabmeat
7 oz/200 g freshly cooked crab claws
5½ oz/150 g canned corn
  kernels, drained
2 tbsp chopped fresh cilantro

TO GARNISH
chopped fresh cilantro
thin strips of lime zest

Heat the oil in a large pan over medium heat. Add the garlic and scallions and cook, stirring, for about 3 minutes, until slightly softened. Add the bell peppers and gingerroot and cook for another 4 minutes, stirring. Pour in the bouillon and season with salt and pepper. Bring to a boil, then lower the heat. Pour in the coconut milk, rice wine, and lime juice, and stir in the grated lime zest and kaffir lime leaves. Simmer for 15 minutes.

Add the crabmeat and crab claws to the soup with the corn and cilantro. Cook the soup for 15 minutes, until the fish is tender and cooked right through.

Remove from the heat and ladle into serving bowls. Garnish with chopped fresh cilantro and strips of lime zest and serve.

seafood soups

spicy won ton soup

easy serves 4

20 minutes 25 minutes

ingredients

2 garlic cloves, chopped
2 scallions, trimmed and chopped
2 tsp light soy sauce
2 tsp sherry
2 tbsp chopped fresh cilantro
2 egg whites
3½ oz/100 g cooked shrimp,
  peeled and chopped
3½ oz/100 g cooked chicken
  meat, chopped
16 won ton wrappers

SOUP
1 tbsp chili oil or sesame oil
3 scallions, trimmed and sliced
1 small red chili, seeded and
  finely chopped
1 red bell pepper, seeded and chopped
4 cups fish bouillon
1 tbsp light soy sauce
2 tbsp sherry
1 tbsp chopped fresh cilantro
1 tbsp chopped fresh parsley

To make the won tons, put the garlic, scallions, soy sauce, sherry, cilantro, and 1 egg white into a large bowl and mix well. Divide the mixture between 2 smaller bowls, then add the shrimp to one bowl and the chicken to the other. Spoon some shrimp mixture into the centers of 8 won ton wrappers, brush around the edges with the remaining egg white, then fold over into triangles and seal well. Take the 2 farthest corners of each triangle and join with egg white. Repeat the process with the remaining 8 won ton wrappers, this time using the chicken mixture.

To make the soup, heat the oil in a large skillet over medium heat. Add the scallions and cook, stirring, for 3 minutes. Add the chili and pepper and cook, stirring, for 5 minutes. Pour in the bouillon, soy sauce, sherry, and herbs. Bring to a boil, lower the heat, and simmer for 10 minutes. Add the won tons. Cook for 5–6 minutes. Remove from the heat, ladle into serving bowls, and serve hot.

shrimp & vegetable bisque

very easy   serves 4

15 minutes   35 minutes
+ 10 minutes
to cool

ingredients

3 tbsp butter

1 garlic clove, chopped

1 onion, sliced

1 carrot, peeled and chopped

1 celery stalk, trimmed and sliced

5 cups fish bouillon

4 tbsp red wine

1 tbsp tomato paste

1 bay leaf

salt and pepper

1 lb 5 oz/600 g shrimp, peeled
  and deveined

scant ½ cup heavy cream

GARNISH

swirls of light cream

whole cooked shrimp

Melt the butter in a large pan over medium heat. Add the garlic and onion and cook, stirring, for 3 minutes, until slightly softened. Add the carrot and celery and cook for another 3 minutes, stirring. Pour in the bouillon and red wine, then add the tomato paste and bay leaf. Season with salt and pepper. Bring to a boil, then lower the heat and simmer for 20 minutes. Remove from the heat and let cool for 10 minutes, then remove and discard the bay leaf.

Transfer half of the soup into a food processor and blend until smooth (you may need to do this in batches). Return to the pan with the rest of the soup. Add the shrimp and cook the soup over low heat for 5–6 minutes.

Stir in the cream and cook for another 2 minutes, then remove from the heat and ladle into serving bowls. Garnish with swirls of light cream and whole cooked shrimp, and serve at once.

The recipes in this section draw on a wide variety of ingredients and dishes from around the world, such as Scotch Broth and Indian Mulligatawny. There is also a Continental-style Salami & Vegetable Chowder, and a Pork & Vegetable Broth bursting with delicious Thai flavors. And for the cost-conscious among you, the Turkey & Lentil Soup provides an excellent way of using leftover turkey during the holidays or at other times during the year. You can also substitute leftover chicken for the turkey whenever the need arises.

poultry &
meat soups

chicken & potato soup with bacon

very easy serves 4

15 minutes 40 minutes

ingredients

1 tbsp butter
2 garlic cloves, chopped
1 onion, sliced
9 oz/250 g smoked lean bacon, chopped
2 large leeks, trimmed and sliced
2 tbsp all-purpose flour
4 cups chicken bouillon
1 lb 12 oz/800 g potatoes, peeled
  and chopped

7 oz/200 g skinless chicken
  breast, chopped
salt and pepper
4 tbsp heavy cream

broiled bacon, chopped, to garnish

fresh crusty rolls, to serve

Melt the butter in a large pan over medium heat. Add the garlic and onion and cook, stirring, for 3 minutes, until slightly softened. Add the chopped bacon and leeks and cook for another 3 minutes, stirring. In a bowl, mix the flour with enough bouillon to make a smooth paste and stir it into the pan. Cook, stirring, for 2 minutes. Pour in the remaining bouillon, then add the potatoes and chicken. Season with salt and pepper. Bring to a boil, then lower the heat and simmer for 25 minutes, until the chicken and potatoes are tender and cooked through.

Stir in the cream and cook for another 2 minutes, then remove from the heat and ladle into serving bowls. Garnish with chopped bacon and serve with fresh crusty rolls.

cream of chicken soup

very easy   serves 4

15 minutes   40 minutes
+ 10 minutes
to cool

ingredients

3 tbsp butter

4 shallots, chopped

1 leek, trimmed and sliced

1 lb/450 g skinless chicken
  breasts, chopped

2½ cups chicken bouillon

1 tbsp chopped fresh parsley

1 tbsp chopped fresh thyme

salt and pepper

¾ cup heavy cream

sprigs of fresh thyme, to garnish

fresh crusty rolls, to serve

Melt the butter in a large pan over medium heat. Add the shallots and cook, stirring, for 3 minutes, until slightly softened. Add the leek and cook for another 5 minutes, stirring. Add the chicken, bouillon, and herbs, and season with salt and pepper. Bring to a boil, then lower the heat and simmer for 25 minutes, until the chicken is tender and cooked through. Remove from the heat and let cool for 10 minutes.

Transfer the soup into a food processor and blend until smooth (you may need to do this in batches). Return the soup to the pan and warm over low heat for 5 minutes.

Stir in the cream and cook for another 2 minutes, then remove from the heat and ladle into serving bowls. Garnish with sprigs of thyme and serve with fresh crusty rolls.

turkey & lentil soup

very easy   serves 4

20 minutes 50 minutes

ingredients

1 tbsp olive oil
1 garlic clove, chopped
1 large onion, chopped
7 oz/200 g mushrooms, sliced
1 red bell pepper, seeded and chopped
6 tomatoes, skinned (see page 8), seeded,
   and chopped
generous 4 cups chicken bouillon
⅔ cup red wine
3 oz/85 g cauliflower florets
1 carrot, peeled and chopped

1 cup red lentils
salt and pepper
12 oz/350 g cooked turkey
   meat, chopped
1 zucchini, trimmed and chopped
1 tbsp shredded fresh basil

fresh basil leaves, to garnish

thick slices of fresh crusty bread,
   to serve

Heat the oil in a large pan. Add the garlic and onion and cook over medium heat, stirring, for 3 minutes, until slightly softened. Add the mushrooms, bell pepper, and tomatoes, and cook for another 5 minutes, stirring. Pour in the bouillon and red wine, then add the cauliflower, carrot, and red lentils. Season with salt and pepper. Bring to a boil, then lower the heat and simmer for 25 minutes, until the vegetables are tender and cooked through.

Add the turkey and zucchini to the pan and cook for 10 minutes. Stir in the shredded basil and cook for another 5 minutes, then remove from the heat and ladle into serving bowls. Garnish with fresh basil leaves and serve with slices of fresh crusty bread.

indian mulligatawny

very easy   serves 4

15–20
minutes   45 minutes

ingredients

2 tbsp vegetable oil
1 garlic clove, chopped
1 large onion, chopped
5½ oz/150 g mushrooms, sliced
2 tbsp all-purpose flour
4 cups chicken bouillon
7 oz/200 g skinless chicken
  breasts, chopped
5½ oz/150 g lean smoked
  ham, chopped
1 carrot, peeled and chopped

5½ oz/150 g potatoes, peeled
  and chopped
1 tbsp curry powder
salt and pepper
1 tbsp chopped fresh cilantro
½ cup heavy cream

GARNISH
grated fresh coconut
sprigs of fresh cilantro
fresh nan bread, to serve

Heat the oil in a large pan. Add the garlic and onion and cook over medium heat, stirring, for 3 minutes, until slightly softened. Add the mushrooms and cook for another 2 minutes. In a bowl, mix the flour with enough bouillon to make a smooth paste, then stir it into the pan. Stir in the remaining bouillon, then add the chicken, smoked ham, carrot, potatoes, and curry powder, and season with salt and pepper. Bring to a boil, then lower the heat and simmer very gently for 30 minutes until the meat and vegetables are tender and cooked through.

Stir in the cilantro and cream and cook for another 5 minutes. Remove from the heat and ladle into serving bowls. Garnish with grated coconut and sprigs of cilantro and serve with nan bread.

salami & vegetable chowder

ingredients

very easy   serves 4

15 minutes   45 minutes

2 tbsp olive oil

1 garlic clove, chopped

1 large onion, chopped

2 tbsp all-purpose flour

4 cups vegetable bouillon

1 lb/450 g potatoes, peeled and sliced

salt and pepper

5½ oz/150 g white cabbage, chopped

1 zucchini, peeled and chopped

2¾ oz/75 g salami, sliced

½ cup heavy cream

fresh crusty rolls, to serve

Heat the oil in a large pan. Add the garlic and onion and cook over medium heat, stirring, for 3 minutes, until slightly softened. In a bowl, mix the flour with enough bouillon to make a smooth paste, then stir it into the pan. Stir in the remaining bouillon, then add the potatoes and season with salt and pepper. Bring to a boil, then lower the heat and simmer for 25 minutes, until the vegetables are tender and cooked through.

Add the cabbage, zucchini, and salami and cook for 10 minutes. Stir in the cream and cook for another 5 minutes. Remove from the heat, ladle into serving bowls and serve with fresh crusty rolls.

beef & cauliflower soup

very easy   serves 4

15–20 minutes   40 minutes

2 tbsp chili oil
1 garlic clove, chopped
3 scallions, trimmed and sliced
1 small red chili, seeded and
  finely chopped
1 red bell pepper, seeded and chopped
4 cups beef bouillon
1 tbsp soy sauce
2 tbsp rice wine or dry sherry
5½ oz/150 g potatoes, peeled
  and chopped

salt and pepper
9 oz/250 g lean beef, sliced
5½ oz/150 g cauliflower florets
4½ oz/125 g broccoli florets

TO SERVE
fresh salad greens
fresh baguette

Heat the oil in a large pan. Add the garlic, scallions, and chili and cook over medium heat, stirring, for 3 minutes, until slightly softened. Add the bell pepper and cook for 5 minutes, stirring. Pour in the bouillon, soy sauce, and rice wine, then add the potatoes and season with salt and pepper. Bring to a boil, then lower the heat and simmer for 15 minutes.

Add the beef, cauliflower, and broccoli and cook for another 15 minutes. Remove from the heat and ladle into serving bowls. Serve with fresh salad greens and fresh baguette.

cheese & bacon soup

very easy   serves 4

15 minutes   40 minutes

ingredients

2 tbsp butter

2 garlic cloves, chopped

1 large onion, sliced

9 oz/250 g smoked lean bacon, chopped

2 large leeks, trimmed and sliced

2 tbsp all-purpose flour

4 cups vegetable bouillon

1 lb/450 g potatoes, peeled
  and chopped

salt and pepper

scant ½ cup heavy cream

3 cups grated colby cheese

grated colby cheese, to garnish

fresh garlic bread, to serve

Melt the butter in a large pan over medium heat. Add the garlic and onion and cook, stirring, for 3 minutes, until slightly softened. Add the chopped bacon and leeks and cook for another 3 minutes, stirring. In a bowl, mix the flour with enough bouillon to make a smooth paste and stir it into the pan. Cook, stirring, for 2 minutes. Pour in the remaining bouillon, then add the potatoes. Season with salt and pepper. Bring the soup to a boil, then lower the heat and simmer gently for 25 minutes, until the potatoes are tender and cooked through.

Stir in the cream and cook for 5 minutes, then gradually stir in the cheese until melted. Remove from the heat and ladle into individual serving bowls. Garnish with grated colby cheese and serve with fresh garlic bread.

pork & vegetable broth

ingredients

very easy   serves 4

15 minutes   45 minutes

1 tbsp chili oil
1 garlic clove, chopped
3 scallions, trimmed and sliced
1 red bell pepper, seeded and
   finely sliced
2 tbsp cornstarch
4 cups vegetable bouillon
1 tbsp soy sauce
2 tbsp rice wine or dry sherry
5½ oz/150 g pork tenderloin, sliced
1 tbsp finely grated lemongrass

1 small red chili, seeded and
   finely chopped
1 tbsp grated fresh gingerroot
salt and pepper
4 oz/115 g fine egg noodles
7 oz/200 g canned water chestnuts,
   drained and sliced

TO SERVE
fresh salad greens
fresh crusty bread

Heat the oil in a large pan. Add the garlic and scallions and cook over medium heat, stirring, for 3 minutes, until slightly softened. Add the bell pepper and cook for another 5 minutes, stirring. In a bowl, mix the cornstarch with enough of the bouillon to make a smooth paste and stir it into the pan. Cook, stirring, for 2 minutes. Stir in the remaining bouillon and the soy sauce and rice wine, then add the pork, lemongrass, chili, and gingerroot. Season with salt and pepper. Bring to a boil, then lower the heat and simmer for 25 minutes.

Bring a separate pan of water to a boil, add the noodles, and cook for 3 minutes. Remove from the heat, drain, then add the noodles to the soup along with the water chestnuts. Cook for another 2 minutes, then remove from the heat and ladle into serving bowls. Serve with fresh salad greens and crusty bread.

sausage & red cabbage soup

very easy   serves 4

15 minutes   50 minutes

2 tbsp olive oil
1 garlic clove, chopped
1 large onion, chopped
1 large leek, trimmed and sliced
2 tbsp cornstarch
4 cups vegetable bouillon
1 lb/450 g potatoes, peeled and sliced
7 oz/200 g skinless sausages, sliced
salt and pepper

5½ oz/150 g red cabbage, chopped
7 oz/200 g canned black-eye
   peas, drained
½ cup heavy cream

ground paprika, to garnish

fresh crusty rolls, to serve

Heat the oil in a large pan. Add the garlic and onion and cook over medium heat, stirring, for 3 minutes, until slightly softened. Add the leek and cook for another 3 minutes, stirring. In a bowl, mix the cornstarch with enough bouillon to make a smooth paste, then stir it into the pan. Cook, stirring, for 2 minutes. Stir in the remaining bouillon, then add the potatoes and sausages. Season with salt and pepper. Bring to a boil, then lower the heat and simmer for 25 minutes.

Add the red cabbage and black-eye peas and cook for 10 minutes, then stir in the cream and cook for another 5 minutes. Remove from the heat and ladle into serving bowls. Garnish with ground paprika and serve with fresh crusty rolls.

scotch broth

very easy   serves 4

20 minutes   1½ hours

ingredients

2¾ oz/75 g pearl barley, rinsed
  and drained
1 tbsp vegetable oil
1 garlic clove, chopped
1 large onion, chopped
1 large leek, trimmed and sliced
generous 4 cups vegetable bouillon
1 bay leaf
1 lb/450 g lean boneless lamb,
  fat trimmed away
salt and pepper

9 oz/250 g potatoes, peeled and sliced
1 large carrot, peeled and chopped
5½ oz/150 g rutabaga, peeled
  and chopped
1 turnip, peeled and chopped
2 celery stalks, trimmed and sliced
2 tsp dried mixed herbs

sprigs of fresh parsley, to garnish

slices of fresh whole-wheat bread,
  to serve

Bring a pan of water to a boil. Add the barley and boil over high heat for 5 minutes, skimming the surface when necessary. Remove from the heat and set aside.

Heat the oil in a large pan. Add the garlic and onion and cook over medium heat, stirring, for 3 minutes, until slightly softened. Add the leek and cook for another 4 minutes, stirring. Stir in the bouillon, then drain the barley and add to the pan along with the bay leaf. Cut the lamb into bite-size chunks and add to the pan. Season with salt and pepper. Bring to a boil, then lower the heat and simmer for 15 minutes. Add the potatoes, carrot, rutabaga, turnip, celery, and mixed herbs and cook for 1 hour.

Remove from the heat, discard the bay leaf, and ladle into serving bowls. Garnish the Scotch broth with sprigs of fresh parsley and serve with slices of fresh whole-wheat bread.

Comforting soups containing beans, grains, and noodles are heartwarming at any time of the year. Many of the recipes in this section use canned beans because they are convenient, but you can use dried if you prefer. Simply adjust the soaking and cooking times accordingly. The times vary according to the type of bean, so always check the instructions on the package. Whether you use canned or dried beans, these soups are highly nutritious, and many need only fresh crusty bread to transform them into satisfying meals in themselves.

beans, grains & noodles

spicy lentil soup

very easy   serves 4

10–15
minutes   50 minutes

ingredients

1 tbsp olive oil

1 onion, sliced

1 leek, trimmed and sliced

scant 5½ cups vegetable bouillon

1 carrot, peeled and chopped

1 celery stalk, trimmed and sliced

generous ⅓ cup brown rice

1 cup red lentils

1 bay leaf

1 tbsp chopped fresh parsley

pinch of saffron threads

1 tsp ground coriander

1 tsp garam masala

salt and pepper

sprigs of fresh cilantro, to garnish

fresh whole-wheat bread, to serve

Heat the oil in a large pan. Add the onion and cook over medium heat, stirring, for 3 minutes, until slightly softened. Add the leek and cook for another 2 minutes, stirring. Stir in the bouillon, then add the carrot, celery, rice, lentils, herbs, and spices. Season with salt and pepper. Bring to a boil, then lower the heat and simmer for 40 minutes until the rice, lentils, and vegetables are tender and cooked through.

Remove the soup from the heat and discard the bay leaf. Ladle into serving bowls, garnish with sprigs of fresh cilantro, and serve with fresh whole-wheat bread.

pea & ham soup

very easy   serves 4

10–15
minutes
+ 10 minutes
to cool

45 minutes

ingredients

1 tbsp butter
1 onion, sliced
1 leek, trimmed and sliced
4 cups vegetable bouillon
1 lb/450 g freshly shelled peas, or frozen
   peas, thawed
7 oz/200 g lean smoked ham, chopped
1 bay leaf

1 tbsp chopped fresh tarragon
salt and pepper
4 tbsp heavy cream

GARNISH
cooked ham, chopped
sprigs of fresh tarragon

fresh crusty rolls, to serve

Melt the butter in a large pan over medium heat. Add the onion and cook, stirring, for 3 minutes, until slightly softened. Add the leek and cook for another 2 minutes, stirring. Stir in the bouillon, then add the peas, ham, bay leaf, and tarragon. Season with salt and pepper. Bring to a boil, then lower the heat and simmer for 30 minutes. Remove from the heat and discard the bay leaf. Let cool for 10 minutes.

Transfer half of the soup into a food processor and blend until smooth. Return to the pan with the rest of the soup, stir in the cream, and cook over low heat for another 5 minutes.

Remove the soup from the heat and ladle into serving bowls. Garnish with chopped ham and sprigs of fresh tarragon and serve with fresh crusty rolls.

soupe au pistou

very easy   serves 4

25 minutes   40 minutes

ingredients

PISTOU SAUCE
scant 1 cup chopped fresh basil
scant ½ cup chopped fresh parsley
3 garlic cloves, finely chopped
5 tbsp extra-virgin olive oil
3 tbsp freshly grated Parmesan

FOR THE SOUP
2 tbsp extra-virgin olive oil
1 garlic clove, finely chopped
1 onion, chopped
5 cups vegetable bouillon

1 lb/450 g potatoes, chopped
3½ oz/100 g thin green beans
1 large carrot, peeled and chopped
7 oz/200 g canned cannellini beans
5½ oz/150 g lean smoked ham, chopped
14 oz/400 g canned tomatoes
1 tbsp chopped fresh thyme
salt and pepper
2¾ oz/75 g dried vermicelli
shavings of fresh Parmesan, to garnish
slices of fresh bread, to serve

To make the pistou, put all the ingredients into a food processor and blend until combined. Transfer into a bowl, cover with plastic wrap, and chill.

To make the soup, heat the oil in a large pan over medium heat. Add the garlic and the onion and cook, stirring, for 3 minutes, until slightly softened. Stir in the bouillon, then add the potatoes, green beans (which have been topped and tailed, then finely chopped), carrot, drained cannellini beans, and ham, and the tomatoes with their juices. Stir in the thyme and season. Bring to a boil, then lower the heat and simmer for 20 minutes. Add the vermicelli and cook for another 12 minutes, or according to the instructions on the package.

Remove from the heat and ladle into serving bowls. Put a generous spoonful of pistou sauce into each bowl, garnish with fresh Parmesan shavings, and serve with slices of fresh bread.

mixed bean soup with swiss cheese

very easy   serves 4

15 minutes   55 minutes
+ 10 minutes
to cool

ingredients

1 tbsp extra-virgin olive oil
3 garlic cloves, finely chopped
4 scallions, trimmed and sliced
7 oz/200 g mushrooms, sliced
4 cups vegetable bouillon
1 large carrot, peeled and chopped
14 oz/400 g canned mixed
   beans, drained
1 lb 12 oz/800 g canned
   chopped tomatoes

1 tbsp chopped fresh thyme
1 tbsp chopped fresh oregano
salt and pepper
6 oz/175 g Swiss cheese, grated
4 tbsp heavy cream

GARNISH
swirls of light cream
finely chopped scallions

thick slices of fresh bread, to serve

Heat the oil in a large pan over medium heat. Add the garlic and scallions and cook, stirring, for 3 minutes, until slightly softened. Add the mushrooms and cook for another 2 minutes, stirring. Stir in the bouillon, then add the carrot, mixed beans, chopped tomatoes, and herbs. Season with salt and pepper. Bring to a boil, then lower the heat and simmer for 30 minutes. Remove from the heat and let cool for 10 minutes.

Transfer into a food processor and blend until smooth. Return to the pan and stir in the cheese. Cook for another 10 minutes, then stir in the cream. Cook for 5 minutes, then remove from the heat and ladle into serving bowls. Garnish with swirls of cream and chopped or sliced scallions. Serve with thick slices of fresh bread.

sweet potato & lentil soup

very easy   serves 4

15–20
minutes +
10 minutes
to cool   55 minutes

ingredients

1 tbsp olive oil

1 garlic clove, chopped

1 large onion, chopped

1 red bell pepper, seeded and chopped

6 tomatoes, skinned (see page 8), seeded
  and chopped

4 cups vegetable bouillon

1 lb/450 g sweet potatoes, peeled
  and chopped

1 carrot, peeled and chopped

1 cup red lentils

salt and pepper

1 tbsp chopped fresh basil

sprigs of fresh basil, to garnish

fresh crusty rolls, to serve

Heat the oil in a large pan. Add the garlic and onion and cook over medium heat, stirring, for 3 minutes, until slightly softened. Add the bell pepper and the tomatoes and cook for another 2 minutes, stirring. Pour in the bouillon, then add the sweet potatoes, carrot, and lentils. Season with salt and pepper. Bring to a boil, then lower the heat and simmer for 30 minutes, until all of the vegetables are tender and cooked through. Remove from the heat and let cool for 10 minutes.

Transfer half of the soup into a food processor and blend until smooth. Return to the pan with the rest of the soup and cook for 10 minutes. Stir in the chopped basil and cook for another 5 minutes. Remove from the heat and ladle into serving bowls. Garnish with sprigs of fresh basil and serve with fresh crusty rolls.

chorizo & red kidney bean soup

very easy   serves 4

15–20 minutes   50 minutes

ingredients

2 tbsp olive oil
2 garlic cloves, chopped
2 red onions, chopped
1 red bell pepper, seeded and chopped
2 tbsp cornstarch
4 cups vegetable bouillon
1 lb/450 g potatoes, peeled, halved, and sliced
salt and pepper

5½ oz/150 g chorizo, sliced
2 zucchini, trimmed and sliced
7 oz/200 g canned red kidney beans, drained
½ cup heavy cream

slices of fresh crusty bread, to serve

Heat the oil in a large pan. Add the garlic and onions and cook over medium heat, stirring, for 3 minutes, until slightly softened. Add the bell pepper and cook for another 3 minutes, stirring. In a bowl, mix the cornstarch with enough bouillon to make a smooth paste and stir it into the pan. Cook, stirring, for 2 minutes. Stir in the remaining bouillon, then add the potatoes and season with salt and pepper. Bring to a boil, then lower the heat and simmer for 25 minutes, until the vegetables are tender.

Add the chorizo, zucchini, and kidney beans to the pan. Cook for 10 minutes, then stir in the cream and cook for another 5 minutes. Remove from the heat and ladle into serving bowls. Serve with slices of fresh crusty bread.

tomato, rice & tarragon soup

very easy   serves 4

20 minutes   50 minutes
+ 10 minutes
to cool

ingredients

2 tbsp olive oil

2 garlic cloves, chopped

2 red onions, chopped

1 red bell pepper, seeded and chopped

8 tomatoes, skinned (see page 8), seeded
  and chopped

4 cups vegetable bouillon

1 celery stalk, trimmed and sliced

generous ¾ cup brown rice

1 tbsp chopped fresh tarragon

salt and pepper

scant ½ cup heavy cream

sprigs of fresh tarragon, to garnish

fresh crusty bread, to serve

Heat the oil in a large pan. Add the garlic and onions and cook over medium heat, stirring, for 3 minutes, until slightly softened. Add the bell pepper and the tomatoes and cook for another 2 minutes, stirring. Stir in the bouillon, then add the celery, rice, and tarragon. Season with salt and pepper. Bring to a boil, then lower the heat and simmer for 30 minutes. Remove from the heat and let cool for 10 minutes.

Transfer half of the soup into a food processor and blend until smooth. Return to the pan with the rest of the soup and cook for 5 minutes. Stir in the cream and cook for another 5 minutes. Remove from the heat and ladle into serving bowls. Garnish with sprigs of fresh tarragon and serve with fresh crusty bread.

chicken, mushroom & barley soup

very easy   serves 4

15 minutes   1½ hours

ingredients

2¾ oz/75 g pearl barley, rinsed
  and drained
2 tbsp butter
1 large onion, sliced
1 large leek, trimmed and sliced
4 cups chicken bouillon
salt and pepper
1 lb/450 g skinless chicken
  breasts, chopped

9 oz/250 g crimini mushrooms, sliced
1 large carrot, peeled and chopped
1 tbsp chopped fresh oregano
1 bay leaf

sprigs of fresh flatleaf parsley,
  to garnish

fresh crusty bread, to serve

Bring a pan of water to a boil. Add the barley and boil over high heat for 5 minutes, skimming the surface when necessary. Remove from the heat and set aside.

Melt the butter in a large pan. Add the onion and cook over medium heat, stirring, for 3 minutes, until slightly softened. Add the leek and cook for another 4 minutes, stirring. Stir in the bouillon, then drain the barley and add to the pan. Season with salt and pepper. Bring to a boil, then lower the heat and simmer for 45 minutes. Add the chicken, mushrooms, carrot, oregano, and bay leaf. Cook for another 30 minutes.

Remove from the heat and discard the bay leaf. Ladle into serving bowls, garnish with sprigs of fresh flatleaf parsley, and serve with fresh crusty bread.

minestrone

easy   serves 4

15–20 minutes   45–50 minutes

ingredients

2 tbsp olive oil
2 garlic cloves, chopped
2 red onions, chopped
2¾ oz/75 g prosciutto, sliced
1 red bell pepper, seeded and chopped
1 orange bell pepper, seeded and chopped
14 oz/400 g canned chopped tomatoes
4 cups vegetable bouillon
1 celery stalk, trimmed and sliced

14 oz/400 g canned borlotti beans, drained
3½ oz/100 g green leafy cabbage, shredded
2¾ oz/75 g frozen peas, thawed
1 tbsp chopped fresh parsley
salt and pepper
2¾ oz/75 g dried vermicelli
freshly grated Parmesan cheese, to garnish
fresh crusty bread, to serve

Heat the oil in a large pan. Add the garlic, onions, and prosciutto and cook over medium heat, stirring, for 3 minutes, until slightly softened. Add the red and orange bell peppers and the chopped tomatoes and cook for another 2 minutes, stirring. Stir in the bouillon, then add the celery, borlotti beans, cabbage, peas, and parsley. Season with salt and pepper. Bring to a boil, then lower the heat and simmer for 30 minutes.

Add the vermicelli to the pan. Cook for another 10–12 minutes, or according to the instructions on the package. Remove from the heat and ladle into serving bowls. Garnish with freshly grated Parmesan and serve with fresh crusty bread.

bean curd & noodle broth

very easy   serves 4

15 minutes   5 minutes

ingredients

1 tbsp sesame oil
1 garlic clove, chopped
4 scallions, trimmed and sliced
1 small red chile, seeded and
  finely chopped
1¼ oz/50 g shiitake mushrooms, sliced
1¼ oz/50 g crimini mushrooms, sliced
1 tbsp rice wine
2 tsp soy sauce
2 tbsp chopped fresh cilantro

4 cups vegetable bouillon
2¾ oz/75 g dried fine egg noodles
3½ oz/100 g firm bean curd, drained and
  cut into small cubes
salt and pepper

chopped fresh cilantro, to garnish

fresh crusty bread, to serve

Heat the oil in a large wok or pan over high heat. Add the garlic, scallions, and chile and stir-fry for 1 minute, until slightly softened. Add the mushrooms, rice wine, soy sauce, cilantro, and bouillon and bring to a boil. Lower the heat, add the noodles, and simmer the soup gently for 3 minutes.

Add the bean curd and season with salt and pepper. Remove from the heat, then transfer into individual serving bowls. Garnish with chopped fresh cilantro and serve with fresh crusty bread.

index